Young Animals and Their Parents

For a free color catalog describing Gareth Stevens' list of high-quality books and multimedia programs, call 1-800-542-2595 (USA) or 1-800-461-9120 (Canada). Gareth Stevens Publishing's Fax: (414) 332-3567.

Library of Congress Cataloging-in-Publication Data available upon request from publisher. Fax: (414) 332-3567 for the attention of the Publishing Records Department.

ISBN 0-8368-2717-1

This North American edition first published in 2000 by
Gareth Stevens Publishing
A World Almanac Education Group Company
330 West Olive Street, Suite 100
Milwaukee, WI 53212 USA

This U.S. edition © 2000 by Gareth Stevens, Inc.
First published as *Ik Lijk Op Mijn Mama* with an original
© 1996 by Mozaïek, an imprint of Uitgeverij Clavis, Hasselt.
Additional end matter © 2000 by Gareth Stevens, Inc.

Text and illustrations: Renne
English translation: Alison Taurel
English text: Dorothy L. Gibbs
Gareth Stevens series editor: Dorothy L. Gibbs
Editorial assistant: Diane Laska-Swanke

Printed in the United States of America

1 2 3 4 5 6 7 8 9 04 03 02 01 00

Young Animals
and Their Parents

Renne

Gareth Stevens Publishing
A WORLD ALMANAC EDUCATION GROUP COMPANY

This little zebra has just been born. It looks a lot like its mother, but they are not exactly the same. Zebras are mammals. They are also herbivores, or animals that eat plants.

A baby zebra has:

1. a smaller and shorter body that still has to grow

2. a tight coat to keep itself warm

3. a shorter and more rounded snout for licking its mother

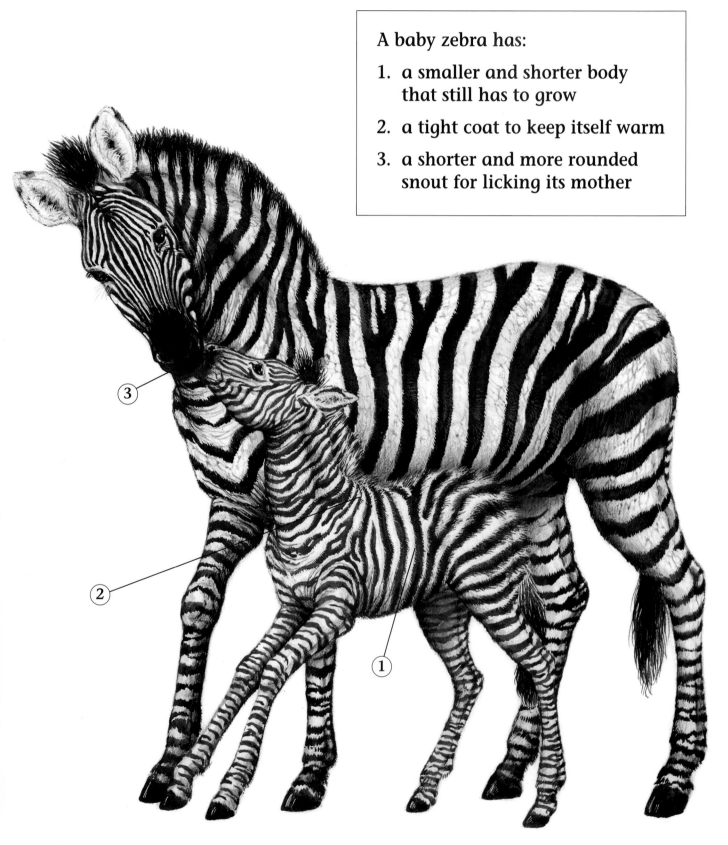

hippopotamuses

giraffes

camels

wild donkeys

Baby herbivores must be able to flee quickly with their mothers to escape from carnivores, or animals that eat meat. Carnivores prey on herbivores. Luckily, the bodies of young herbivores are well developed. They look a lot like their parents.

Some differences, however, between young mammals and their parents are essential. For example, the color of their fur helps some young animals hide in their surroundings.

red deer fawn

cheetah kitten

Adult males often have distinct features, such as horns, a mane, or bright colors. If their young looked that way, the fathers might see them as enemies and attack them. If the young had antlers, fangs, or horns, they might accidentally injure their mothers.

Young mammals that must live out in the open are very well developed when they are born. Most mammals born in hidden burrows come into the world hairless, blind, and defenseless.

Rabbits are born in burrows — well hidden.

Hares are born in a grassy meadow — without shelter.

These baby animals need a nice cozy nest.

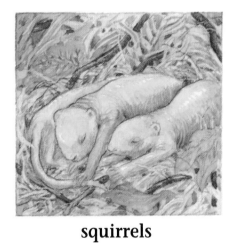

squirrels

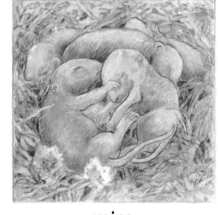

mice

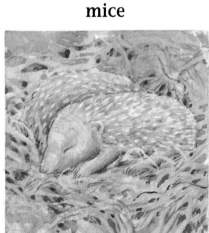

muskrats

hedgehogs

Most young carnivores stay inside a safe cave all day.

wolves

otters

red foxes

badgers

lynx

pine martens

Bear cubs are born during their mother's winter hibernation, and they are very small. With only her reserves of fat to live on at this time, the mother bear could not feed the cubs if they were larger.

brown bears

ferrets

ermines

These young mammals have grown up a lot.

1. brown bear
2. spotted hyena
3. polar bear
4. American black bear
5. golden jackal

6. giant panda
7. lynx
8. red fox
9. leopard
10. wolf
11. tiger
12. cougar
13. jaguar
14. wild cat
15. lion
16. cheetah
17. raccoon
18. wolverine
19. otter
20. ferret
21. genet
22. ermine
23. weasel

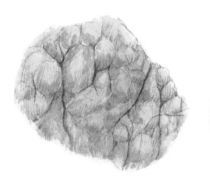

skin of
an adult
walrus

coat of
a young
walrus

skin of
an adult
sea lion

coat of
a young
sea lion

adult grey seal and seal pup

Sea mammals, such as seals, sea lions, and walruses, have a thick layer of fat under their skin to protect them from the cold. Their young are born with a warm, woolly coat because they do not yet have a layer of fat.

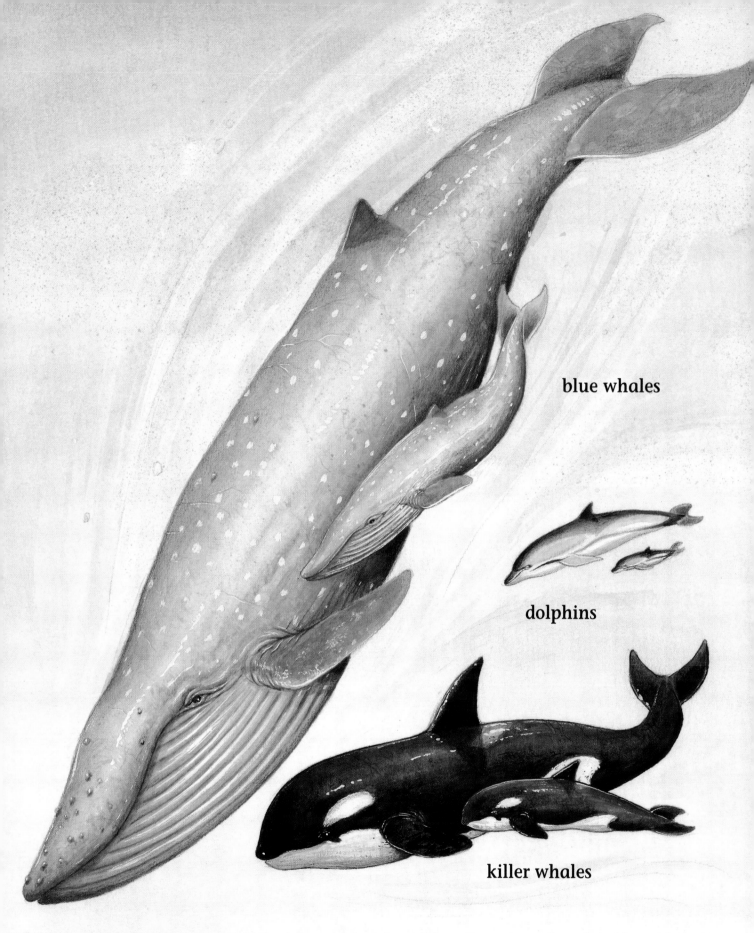

blue whales

dolphins

killer whales

Like many other young mammals, a young sea mammal must lead almost exactly the same life as its mother from the time it is born, so it looks almost exactly like her.

Monkeys and apes are primates, which are the kinds of mammals that most resemble human beings.

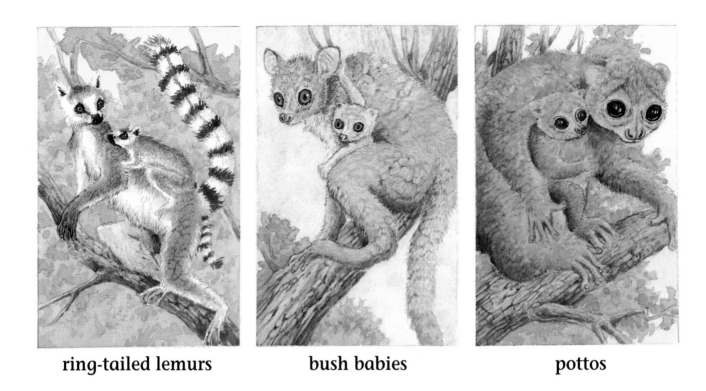

| ring-tailed lemurs | bush babies | pottos |

Apes generally are more developed than monkeys, but, at birth, both are weak and have almost no hair. Their mothers look after them and protect them for a long time.

rhesus monkeys   golden spider monkeys   squirrel monkeys

As they grow, young monkeys and apes look more and more like their parents. In some species, adult males look distinctly different than females and young ones. They have special features that make them easy to recognize.

The adult male baboon has a long, strong snout.

The adult male gorilla has silver-gray fur on its back.

The adult male mandrill has very bright colors on its face.

The cheeks of an adult male orangutan grow to be very wide.

Something very special happens when kangaroos are born. A baby kangaroo develops mostly outside its mother's body in a warm pocket called a pouch. Although very small and weak, a newborn kangaroo climbs into the pouch by itself.

A newborn kangaroo

climbs toward its mother's pouch

and, once inside, attaches itself to a nipple for feeding.

When the young kangaroo is too large for the pouch, it leaves it for good.

All marsupials are born and develop the same way kangaroos do. This little koala is about six months old.

Platypuses are born in an even more unusual way. Platypuses lay eggs — like birds! Like other mammals, however, they suckle their young.

A baby platypus looks like a little worm.

A baby bird does not look like its mother at all.
When it is born, it is not fully developed.
The egg is too small for a baby bird
to develop completely inside it.

The newborn is covered with a thin layer of down,
and it cries loudly for food. When the baby bird
gets enough food, it grows very quickly.

Some baby birds stay in a nest until they are able to fly. These babies are well cared for and protected in the nest.

This is the nest of a long-tailed tit.

Other young birds, however, are able to leave their nests very quickly. The ostrich is a good example of this kind of bird.

Ostriches are born with a downy coat that protects them against the cold, and, because the color of their feathers blends so well with the landscape, the young are barely noticeable.

Although these young birds do not look much like their parents, they each have a distinct feature that identifies the species to which they belong.

From an early age, the avocet has a curved beak.

Even a young mute swan has a long neck.

Great bustards, both young and adult, have powerful feet.

Everyone recognizes baby reptiles, because they look exactly like their parents.

They need to have the same features as their parents because few adult reptiles take care of their young. As soon as baby reptiles hatch, they have to take care of themselves.

Like baby reptiles, baby amphibians also hatch from eggs, but the young emerge as larvae. Although adult amphibians can live as easily on land as in the water, the larvae can breathe only underwater.

Young amphibians live differently than their parents, so they look different.

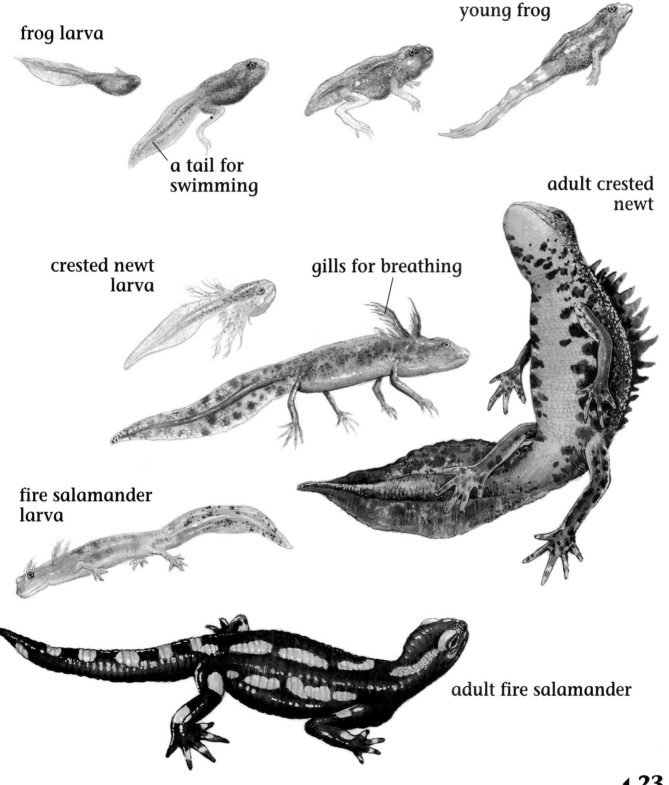

young frog

frog larva

a tail for swimming

adult crested newt

crested newt larva

gills for breathing

fire salamander larva

adult fire salamander

These are insect larvae and the adult insects into which they develop.

1. longhorn beetle
2. spruce bark beetle
3. yellow jacket
4. stag beetle
5. burying beetle
6. rhinoceros beetle
7. pine weevil
8. spittlebug
9. alpine beetle
10. earwig
11. cockchafer
12. dung beetle

After insect larvae hatch, they change form several times
as they grow. These changes are known as metamorphosis.

13. grasshopper
14. ant lion
15. carabus beetle
16. bumblebee
17. ladybug
18. aphids
19. green lacewing
20. water beetle
21. dragonfly
22. spinning
    water beetle
23. caddis fly

Insect larvae often live in different surroundings than their parents, which is why they look so different. The larvae of butterflies and moths are good examples.

7. cinnabar moth
8. swallowtail butterfly
9. drinker moth
10. garden tiger moth
11. six-spot burnet moth
12. large blue butterfly

1. iron prominent moth
2. ring silkmoth
3. puss moth
4. lesser purple emperor butterfly
5. painted lady butterfly
6. small tortoiseshell butterfly

Most insect larvae do not look like adult insects at all, but some look a little like their parents. Sometimes all they lack are wings.

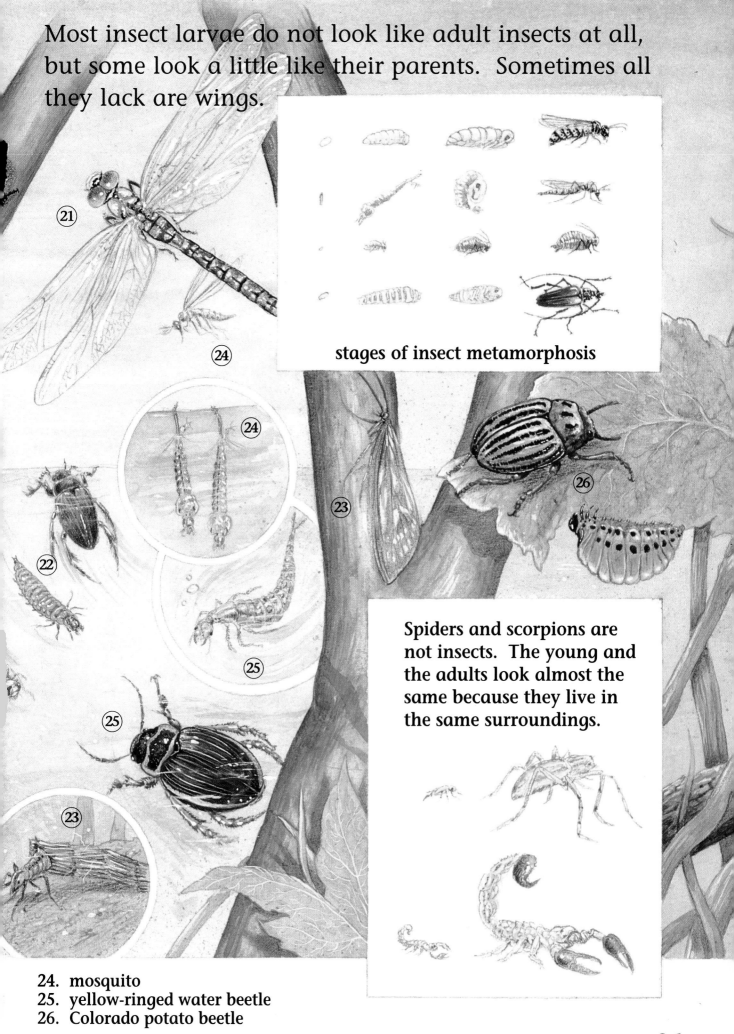

stages of insect metamorphosis

Spiders and scorpions are not insects. The young and the adults look almost the same because they live in the same surroundings.

24. mosquito
25. yellow-ringed water beetle
26. Colorado potato beetle

13. death's head sphinx moth
14. currant moth
15. elm spanworm moth

Many sea creatures begin life as larvae, too.
Most baby fish have to change a lot before they
look like their mothers. Of course, there are exceptions.

Some fish, such as sea horses, are fully developed when they are born. The same is true for sharks. Most sharks give birth to their young instead of laying eggs.

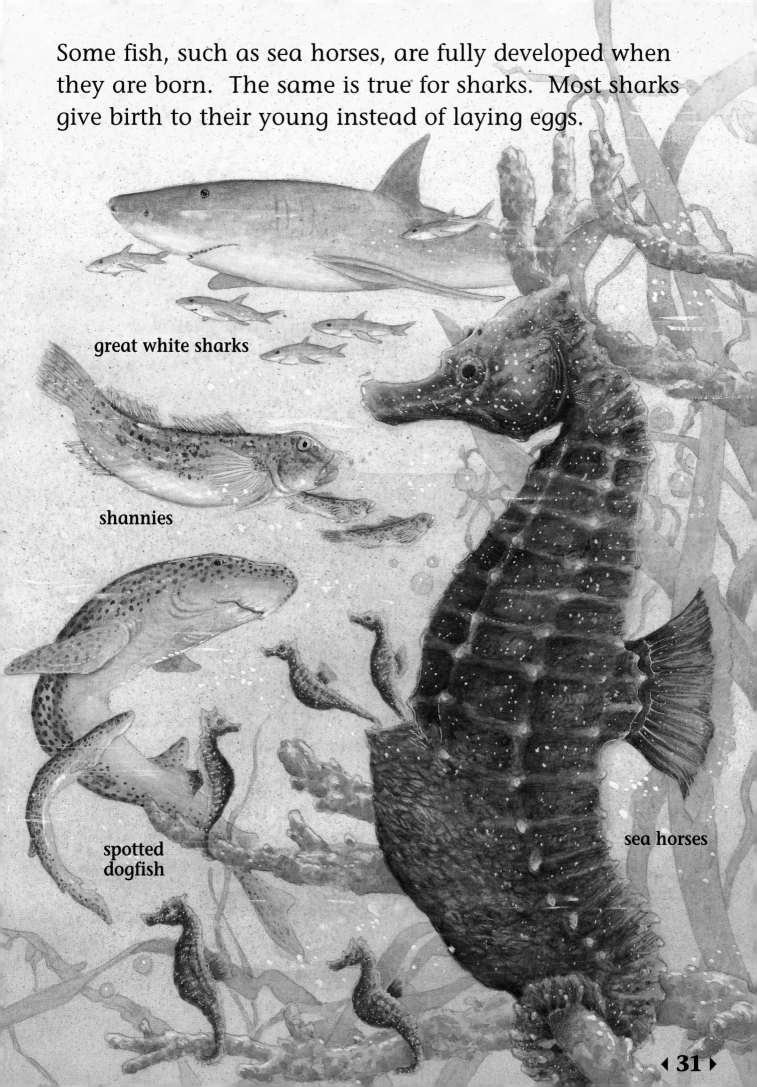

great white sharks

shannies

spotted
dogfish

sea horses

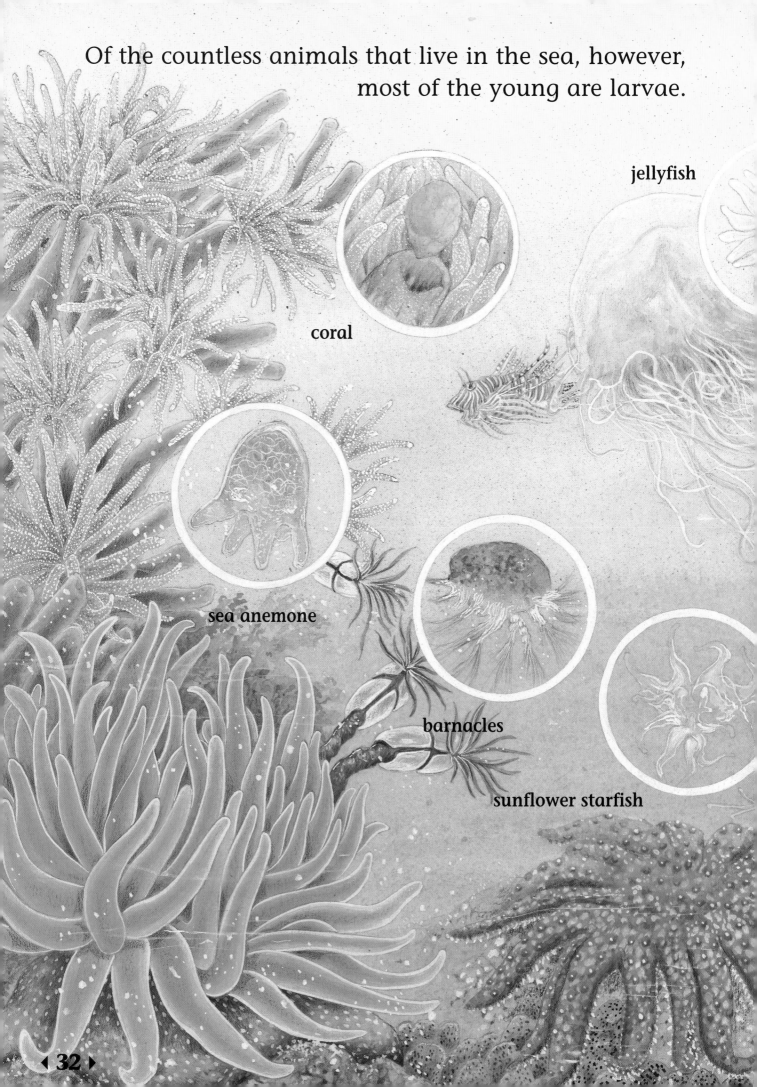

Of the countless animals that live in the sea, however,
most of the young are larvae.

jellyfish

coral

sea anemone

barnacles

sunflower starfish

The larvae of fish, shellfish, and mollusks are also known as plankton. Plankton is an important food source for larger sea animals.

brittle star

Mollusks such as squid and octopuses are well developed when they are born. Because the young live in the open sea like their parents, they look a lot like their parents.

crab

hermit crab

sea urchin   dog whelk

Why don't all young animals look the same as their parents?
The way they live and grow determines how they look.

crane fly

comma butterfly
and caterpillars

currant moth
caterpillar

green lacewing

fall webworm

jay

bee beetle

lynx

bumblebee

Nature provides many different ways to help young animals of all kinds survive, become adults, and, eventually, have young of their own.

great tits

currant moth

viviparous lizard

deer

large white butterfly caterpillars

orange tip butterfly

leaf beetle

crab spider

wood snails

Glossary

amphibian: an animal that is able to live either on land or in the water. A frog is an amphibian. Adult amphibians usually breathe air with lungs; young amphibians, or larvae, usually have gills and can breathe only in water.

birth: (n) the appearance of new life coming directly out of the body of its mother; give birth to: (v) to produce young that are alive when they come out of their mother's body, instead of developing in and hatching from an egg.

emerge: to come out and be seen, usually after being covered or hidden inside something. When a chicken hatches, it emerges from inside its eggshell.

hatch: to come into the world, or be born, by coming out of an egg. The young of birds, fish, and many insects hatch from eggs.

hibernation: a long, inactive period at certain times of the year, usually winter, through which some animals rest or sleep.

larva: (plural: larvae) the wormlike form of most young insects, and some other animals without a backbone, at the time they hatch. A caterpillar is the larva of a butterfly or a moth. A tadpole is the larva of a frog.

mammal: an animal with a backbone and hair or fur on its body. A female mammal usually gives birth to live young and feeds them with milk from her body.

marsupials: a group of mammals in which females carry their young in a pouch on the outside of their abdomens. Kangaroos and koalas are two well-known marsupials.

metamorphosis: a series of changes in form and appearance that some animals go through as they grow, from the time they are born or hatch until they become adults. A butterfly changes from an egg, to a caterpillar (larva), to a pupa, before becoming an adult insect.

plankton: the tiny plants and animals that float around in bodies of water. Tiny plants with no roots, leaves, or stems, such as algae, are called vegetable plankton. Very small animals, such as fish larvae, are called animal plankton.

prey: (v) to hunt animals for food. Usually larger animals prey on smaller animals. Owls often prey on mice. Wolves will sometimes hunt larger animals, such as deer.

reptile: an air-breathing animal that has a backbone and, usually, slimy or scaly skin. A reptile moves by sliding on its belly, like a snake, or crawling along on very short legs, like a lizard.

reserves: supplies that are stored, held back, or set aside to be used later or in a time of special need.

suckle: to feed with the milk of a mother animal directly from her body. Baby mammals drink their mother's milk from a nipple on her body.

More Books to Read

50 Animal Mothers and Babies.
   Molly Walsh (McClanahan Books)

Animal Dads. Sneed B. Collard III
   (Houghton Mifflin)

Animal Lives. Nature's Hidden Worlds
   (series). Cecilia Fitzsimons
   (Raintree/Steck-Vaughn)

Animal Relationships. Animal Survival
   (series). Michel Barré
   (Gareth Stevens)

Baby Animals. Extraordinary Animals
   (series). Andrew Brown (Crabtree)

Baby Birds: Growing and Flying.
   Secrets of the Animal World (series).
   Eulalia García (Gareth Stevens)

Bringing Up Baby: Wild Animal
   Families. Animal Planet (series).
   Discovery Communications
   (Crown)

Kangaroos: Animals with a Pouch.
   Secrets of the Animal World (series).
   Andreu Llamas (Gareth Stevens)

Welcome to the World of Animals
   (series). Diane Swanson
   (Gareth Stevens)

Videos

America's Wild Baby Animals.
   (Schoolhouse Video)

Animal Families: Mother Nature.
   (Questar, Inc.)

Baby Animals at Play: Babies of the Wild.
   (Madacy Entertainment Group)

Bush Babies. (AIT: Agency for
   Instructional Technology)

Mothers of the Wild. Young of the
   Wild Collection Set. (BFS Video)

Young of the Wild. Baby Animals.
   (BFS Video)

Web Sites

Names of Animals, Babies,
   and Groups of Animals.
   www.EnchantedLearning.com/subjects/
   animals/Animalbabies.shtml

Nest-Cam! *www.icehouse.net/erickw/*
   nestcam/wwwnestcam.html

Birth Sequence: Female giraffe calf.
   www.cmzoo.org/commentary.html

The Spockies: The Dr. Spock Special
   Honors for Animal Parents.
   www.discovery.com/stories/nature/
   animalfamilies/animalfamilies.html

To find additional Web sites, use a reliable search engine with one or more
of the following keywords: *amphibians, animal parents, baby animals,*
carnivores, herbivores, insects, larvae, mammals, marsupials, nests, and *reptiles.*

Index